Ade Durojaiye

I0168450

YOU**CAN**
open
your
eyes
NOW

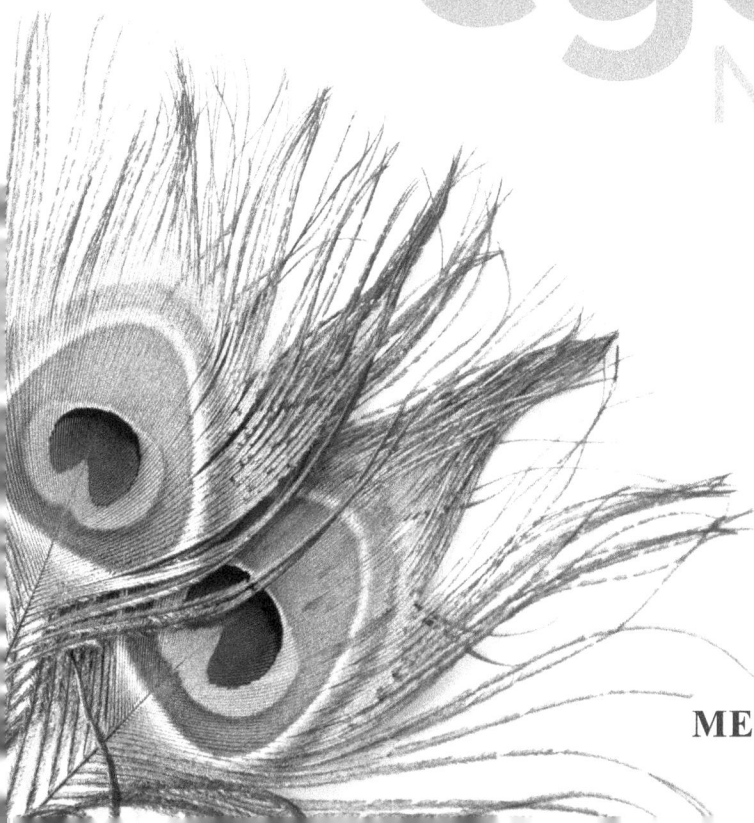

MEGAS SEIRIOS
Publications

ADE DUROJAIYE
YOU CAN OPEN YOUR EYES NOW
1ˢᵗ EDITION 2015

ISBN: 978-960-7350-94-7

This book is published by **Megas Seirios Publications**, founded by the **Servers' Society Spiritual Centre** based in Athens, Greece. To find more information about the mission, works and activities of the Society and/or to place an order, please visit our website:
www.megas-seirios.com

or contact us at:
9, Sarantaporou Street, Athens, Greece, P.O.: 111 44
e-mail: info@megas-seirios.com
Tel.: +30 210 20 15 194
Tel./Fax: +30 210 22 30 864

Cover and book design: Marianna Smyrniotou

Dedicated
to the Master Dimitris Kakalidis
and his Disciples.

☙

acknowledgements

I wish to express my profound gratitude to
Andreas Dritsas and Voula Kostopetrou,
who lovingly contributed to the realisation of this book.

 C3

CONTENTS

The painting

The night was still young at the Center although it was already 10pm. Alex had just finished his group. He and some of its members filed one behind the other into the kitchen. Some helping themselves to cold water from the fridge. Others to the homemade chocolate candy in the two boxes left on the worktop. There in the kitchen they gathered for a little while before saying their goodbyes.

Alex had nothing else planned for the day and was going to remain at the Center until everyone left. He was used to doing that now, staying until the very end, sometimes up until 3 or 4am. He liked the open discussions, which usually took place after the groups.

Alex was still in the kitchen when Despina walked in. She too had just finished her group. But unlike Alex's, most of hers had left immediately after. Despina was also fond of staying late whenever she could. Together they walked down the stairs leading from the kitchen into the courtyard below.

In front of them was a painting of a rocky river in autumn, flanked by slender tree trunks and colourful flowers, flowing gracefully through the dense forest. The painting was in the middle of the courtyard and was the first thing seen when one walked down into the bright but warm space. The painting was a new addition to the recently completed courtyard.

On the white sofa directly underneath the painting was Andreas, talking to some seven people, all seated in a circle around the sofa. Alex and Despina made the total number nine. Both sat to the left of Andreas, Despina on the director's chair and Alex on a cushioned chair.

Andreas was the Head of Omilos Eksipiretiton (The Servers' Society), as the Center was officially known. He had decided to take the responsibility of heading the Society through the agreement, consistent support and encouragement of the Master, the founder of the Society, making it possible for the teachings of the Master and work of the Society to carry on following his passing. It was thus through Andreas and the other older disciples that Alex and the newer members of the Society now received the teachings given by the Master.

For Andreas, the teachings were proven many times in his life. "I never accepted anything just like that," he used to say to Alex and the others. "I always wanted to have it proven in practice, in my daily life, have a personal experience. So I would go home and meditate, write, do everything the Master said. And each time, the results in my everyday life proved the teachings to be true."

And it was this personal experience of the teachings that Andreas shared with the members of the Society.

"We have to express our Higher Self and be in the flow of life," he said.

Andreas spoke with a certain voice. You got the sense he knew what he was talking about from his personal experience. His words were firm but full of love, like the river flowing behind him.

"Resistance to life brings pain and illness, a natural reaction when we hold back," he continued. Then, "Where is Kiriakos?"

"Upstairs in the computer room," Despina said.

"Hiding is he? Kidding himself he is doing something?"

Andreas was one of those people who told you how it was to the point that you either tried to distance yourself or go unnoticed. Both of which were impossible since he was always asking after your welfare and besides, behind the stern perception people had of him, you knew deep down he cared for you regardless.

Andreas said, "When you are upset with someone and you don't do something about it by letting them know, then you keep the upset emotions in your stomach. This emotion is kept against its will and because it has no way to get out it starts to cause pain. Like an angry man locked in a cage, who wants to get out but he can't so he starts punching the walls of his cell."

At that moment Kiriakos walked into the room. "Welcome!" Andreas said. "Found anything in the computer of use to us here? Any new gadget we can while away our time with?"

Kiriakos was hesitant in replying, knowing it was a rhetorical question. Alex's eyes were on Kiriakos but his mind was thinking about the angry man locked in a cell. He knew him well. He was like him, walking around the place with pent up anger towards his ex-girlfriend and his life in Greece. And he wouldn't talk to anyone about it. Despina was quiet until she motioned Kiriakos towards the chair beside her.

Alex wasn't naturally talkative, but now the situation was worse; he was afraid of letting anyone in and would not talk except when necessary. But the more he listened, the more he understood where he had been going wrong and where all his pain was coming from: not expressing himself. Andreas told them life was about expression.

"The universe is always expressing," he said, "constantly flowing. And since you are a part of the process, you have to do the same, express and flow like life itself."

Despina had her own issues. And like Alex was also new. She'd first come with Vasiliki for one of the theatrical plays held by the Center. Vasiliki and her worked at the psychiatric hospital in Dafni and were close friends. She had heard a lot about what went on there and how it was helping her friend. It was not until eighteen months before, however, when she was struggling in her relationship with her parents, that she'd finally decided on taking up the services of the Center.

Andreas carried on by saying humans lived in a constant war, when in reality there was nothing to fight over since all people were a reflection of the Self, and were responding to their own needs.

Really?! There is nothing to fight over? Despina thought, finding it difficult to accept the notion. Don't we have to fight for ourselves? Won't people walk all over you if you don't fight your corner? What does he mean all people are a reflection of the Self? Despina had many questions running through her mind but could not bring herself to ask them, ironically going against the night's teachings.

Andreas talked about other things too, but Alex had heard what he came to hear that night. Now it was up to him to do something about it.

Despina typically liked to digest what she heard, though, process her thoughts first before saying anything. Ironically, expressing herself was what had created the trouble within her family in the first place, at least so she thought as they packed up for the night. "Every time I say something, it seems to come out wrong," she said to herself.

"What do you think?" Alex asked Despina as they walked out. "I feel lucky to have found a place like the Center", he said, before she could answer. "I no longer feel alone with life's problems".

Despina nodded in agreement about finding such a place but she was less clear about some of the things they'd discussed.

"I have lots of questions in my head, I need further clarity so I can understand" she concluded.

When it rains

It looked blue-black outside. Alex was sitting in the kitchen drinking his cup of Greek coffee when he suddenly stood up and walked towards the balcony. He leaned on the glass door and watched as the trees were tossed left and right by the wind. The rain was so heavy he could barely see the houses on the opposite side of the street.

Unlike some of his friends who complained about rain and its so-called disruption to their lives, Alex loved the smell of rain, the coolness of the air, and the sound of raindrops. It reminded him of when he used to play with his brother Peter in the rain.

When it rained, they would go outside to dance in it and run around the compound, jumping and kicking puddle, or pretend to be under waterfalls by standing under the downspout from the roof. "You children will catch a cold," their mother would cry out anxiously. Of course they did catch a cold at one time or another, but this did not stop them playing in the rain the next time it fell.

Alex was shy of forty now, so dancing in the rain was no longer something he did, not without his beloved brother anyway. He drank the rest of his coffee and placed the cup in the sink, then went into the bedroom to put on his robe. His eyes were still on the rain as he walked back to the breakfast bar in the kitchen.

Two things happened when it rained heavily in Athens. The streets with their slopes became a swift-running river carrying with it all of the rubbish of the city. This meant although the streets were now somewhat washed, the mess of the city was also more obvious and needed to be cleared away when the rain stopped.

Today's rain seemed to be telling Alex something as he stared at the floating garbage. "What a mess", he thought to himself. Suddenly Athena flashed before his mind coated in anger and fury.

"I am not in love anymore. I want to experience life before I settle down" she said.

16

Even though all she bragged about with her friends was all the interesting things we were up to. What an excuse! he thought. Alex was seeing his own emotional baggage brought to the surface. Baggage which had been buried for longer than necessary and was now coming up for him to do something about.

Then he remembered what had happened the night before. He had been out with his friends for dinner and before heading home decided to make a stop at the Center. It was now a part of his daily routine and he felt better for it too. Unusually for a Saturday evening, there were many people in the building when he arrived.

Apart from one or two people, everyone else was in the courtyard. He could not find a chair to sit on so settled on the concrete plinth next to the plants.

"What is the discussion about?" he leaned over to Maria quietly.

"I haven't got a clear picture myself, I have just arrived too," she said.

"Acceptance", whispered Kyriakos who was sitting beside Maria.

Alex sat upright, supporting himself with both hands stretched out on the plinth. Andreas was in a white long-sleeved shirt with blue horizontal stripes. His speckled grey hair was just about thick enough to hide the temple of his rimless eyeglass. Acceptance, he told them, was non-resistance to reality. "People are ill because they want the world to work according to their rules," he said.

"Imagine the amount of chaos that comes from such expectations. Not only do you stress yourself, you also put a strain on others through this expectation" he continued. "By the way are you eating? What have you eaten today?" This question was directed at Alex.

"Yes," replied Alex. "Grilled pork chops, potatoes, and salad. And some bread too," he added.

"You can't have eaten much, since it doesn't show. You need to eat larger quantities so you can gain weight and have the strength to do things," said Andreas.

He carried on, "As long as there is no resistance to an objective situation, the mind is free from negative thoughts and is able to function properly." Though he was addressing the group, it seemed he was still talking to Alex. This was something everyone at the Center was now accustomed to, the idea of "The Group" and "The Individual" being the same.

Alex found this way of viewing life a key aspect of the Center's teaching. On the surface, it could be easily overlooked, but when understood deeply, it meant being aware that the individual represented the group and vice versa. It meant seeing yourself in the other. Understanding their many aspects are also within us even if we choose not to express it. Since union with our fellow man and the world brought about deeper awareness and harmony.

Alex was struggling to make sense of what Andreas was saying. What does he mean by acceptance? he thought. "Andreas, are you saying we shouldn't have expectations, that we should accept everything?" Alex blurted out uncontrollably.

"Expectation brings attachment. And attachment leads to disharmony. If you are attached to the outcome of something then you put yourself in a position of dependence".

Then Andreas uttered the words that finally got to him: "For example, you are trying to bury the hurt and pains of the past while expecting to be well. This is impossible! You have to accept whatever happened, not passively, but with awareness and love."

"How can I accept what Athena did? How will I?" He murmured under his breath. There in the kitchen he recalled his feelings from the night before.

Suddenly, the words popped into his head: "There is no right or wrong action, only conscious and unconscious." They kept replaying in his mind as if to make sure he grasped what they meant.

The resentment Alex had towards Athena swelled up inside him until teardrops trickled down his cheeks. Transforming the anger into forgiveness, for himself and Athena. Then there was a sense of complete acceptance of what had happened between them. The harsh words they had spoken to each other and everything else. All was coming to the surface now. And being washed away in a current of acceptance.

There is nobody at home

Things had looked so promising when Despina started dating Alex after their meeting at the Center. They used to talk and laugh about everything. But not anymore. Now, all Alex did was mope around the place. Despina was a warm-hearted girl with a cheery disposition, and at first tried to use this to get Alex out of his dark moods.

Frustrated and unable to bear Alex's moodiness, she spoke up as they sat in the living room watching TV, each at one end of the sofa. "We have a problem. It seems your lights are out."

"What do you mean?" Alex asked.

"I can't see any signs of someone living here. Can't you see?"

"No, I can't," Alex said, "and I really don't understand what you mean by my 'lights are out'."

On the surface, Alex appeared to have it all together. But in reality, he had created a façade that enabled him to bury his feelings. The split from his long-term relationship with Athena was still raw. He had not seen the break up coming, and so was devastated when it happened. His whole world seemed to have crumbled around him. All he wanted was to be swallowed up by the earth.

Alex and Athena had just moved to Athens. She moved three months ahead of him so she could find them a home and prepare the grounds for the big change. They were both tired of the grey British weather and had been talking about moving back to Greece for a while. So when Athena lost her job as an architect in a small practice, they used the opportunity to follow through with their dream.

Alex worked as an engineer and earned quite a good salary as a consultant. However, the thought of losing such a lucrative job did not put him off. He was keen on moving, and excited about the prospects of a new life in Greece. Going to the beach on warm sunny days was no longer going to be something they did when on summer holidays.

Like every couple they had their rough patches but always made up before the day was over. This time it was different. The disagreement was proving troublesome, as days turned into weeks.

"It's not working," she told him one evening.

Confused, he asked, "What's not working? What are you talking about?"

Athena wanted out, and Alex could not understand why. He had done everything for her, or so he thought. He got on well with her family and friends too, which was not an easy feat for a Greek family, considering everybody is in each other's lives and business, all the time. But for Alex, having Athena's family in their business wasn't a problem. Ironically, it was a source of joy and support.

This made it more difficult for him. "When and where did it all go wrong?" he kept asking himself. The beautiful life they dreamt about had met a premature death. He could not believe how quickly everything changed.

When he wasn't at work, he was at home, on his sofa or bed with hands crossed behind his head. The curtains were closed most days with very little light coming into the small flat he was renting in Ag. Paraskevi. He had become withdrawn and melancholic. The hurt seemed too great to bear; how to stop his heart from beating had become a daily pre-occupation.

Everything changed when his phone rang one Sunday afternoon. It was Yiannis, calling from London. Yiannis and Alex went back a long way. Yiannis had been calling every so often to check on his friend ever since the break up with Athena. But this call was a special one, the most important, and it came at the right time too, because he was able to talk Alex out of his suicidal thoughts. Had it been a day late the story may have been different.

Eighteen months later and Alex was still struggling, not with his grim thoughts, but with living life again. Days had passed and Alex was thinking about his conversation with Despina. He knew somehow that Despina was right but it wasn't very clear why. She didn't say more either, leaving him to take in her few words. Later on that evening he decided to go to the Center.

The neighbourhood was busy with cars and people. There was a local basketball tournament on so all the parking spots were taken. He had just driven round the block a second time when a car pulled out from a spot right outside the Center, allowing Alex to park his car. He walked up the stairs, leaned over the flowers on the ledge, taking in a whiff of their scent, before pressing the bell.

The front room was pretty much empty. Everyone was in the courtyard. Alex treated everyone to a general greeting as he walked down the stairs. He then leaned against the wall beside them, his hands crossed behind his back. Andreas was sitting in his usual spot and was talking to them about life when Alex somehow switched off the lights which were behind his back.

He turned frantically to switch them back on as the voice from the sofa said, "Aha! Alex, I see the lights are off and there is nobody at home."

"No, my hands hit the switch by mistake," Alex said.

"Oh Alex," Andreas said in his stern but embracing voice. "You still don't understand. Let me tell you... You should know by now that things don't just happen. Everything is connected."

He had heard those words before and had even said it in the past on numerous occasions, but Alex had never really grasped their deeper meaning. And that was one of the beautiful things about going to the Center, being able to open up and go beyond the confined ideas and principles that you have learned to live your life with.

"At the moment you are the walking dead, you have switched off the lights within you because of what one girl did to you in the past. There is no life in you, no zest, it is all empty." Andreas always joked that he was the meanest person around according to some of those attending the Center, and it was easy to see why people thought that way. But they couldn't be further from the truth. Alex had not met anyone else who loved him without any sugar-coating.

"You cannot be well if there is no life in you. Everything around you is not working because there is no life in it to make it work." Then Andreas turned to the rest of the people in the courtyard and said, "Life is for living in

the present moment, not for crying over the past or worrying over the future. To live is to give 100% to all you do.
And to do that one needs to have passion."

Alex could not speak; he had been ripped apart in a
loving way. And though it was painful to hear, he understood that it was all true. Andreas was right and so
was Despina. Although he was over Athena, he had never
gone back to living again. He merely existed. He had become afraid; living for him meant getting hurt and he
didn't want that to happen again.

His drive to Despina's home that night was slow as he
used the time to process the images and thoughts flash-
ing through his mind. He pulled up in front of the house
then switched off the engine. And there in the dark of
night he realized he was causing more pain to himself
than Athena had ever done.

"Despina!" he called out as he opened the door. "I am
sorry. I know I am trying to protect myself but I am also
stopping myself from living. I am no longer going to im-
prison myself. And you deserve better too."

"You shouldn't be sorry. I know why you are afraid.
Everything will be fine", she said.

Things fall apart

It has been three months since CPG closed. Alex was now working with Maria, Helen and Panos. They had maintained their bond and trust for each other but the closing of the office and the manner in which it happened had affected them all. Helen and Panos were especially angry and most times bitter about it. Alex was upset too, but the influence and teaching received from the Center helped. He could see why and where everything went wrong. He could also see the difference practising what he learnt made to him.

The last weeks before the final close of the office as they knew it was difficult for everyone. The air was tense with lots of awkward moments. Kostas tried his best to come across neutral, but it was too late. The damage had already been done and Helen made sure he knew it.

CPG was in the commercial district of Marousi on the top floor of a ten-story building. It was an open and airy office flooded with light. It had great views too, and on a clear day one could see the port of Piraeus. It was from here the family worked day in day out for one another. They had moved there five years ago, from a much smaller and expensive office a few blocks away. And back then there wasn't the unity they had until now.

Nikos and Katerina ran CPG. Nikos was a former insurance broker, while Katerina his wife had come from a retail background. Katerina's family had settled in the area about fifty years ago, when it was not yet developed. She had owned a designer clothing store before starting the business with Niko, and so knew quite a lot of people, which was useful for everyone in the office.

With them were Alex, Kostas, Maria, Helen and Panos. CPG was in the real estate business, and it had a good reputation too because the team worked together, trusted each other and had a strong family bond which was easily perceived by a client. That was until Nikos and Katerina decided to change everything, forgetting what had made CPG successful and strong in the first place.

What made mattered worse was Kostas knew what was coming. They all knew Kostas was Nikos' and Katerina's favourite. But it was still a blow for the others to learn that consideration was not given to the group. Nikos, it appeared, had some financial issues which were becoming unbearable. To solve the problem the three decided to change the commission structure, relocate the office to the basement of Niko's house, while still changing an office fee.

All of a sudden the family unit had been broken. They were not related by blood but by thought and action. Until now, they had stuck together and acted as one and because of that they had weathered the storms of the past, closing deals even when market conditions were poor. But now everything seemed different. Nikos and Katerina were out to protect themselves at the expense of everybody else. The group and its strength in unity was no longer important.

"What do they think. That we are going to pay to work from their basement? I can work from my home," Helen said angrily.

"I don't mind working from the basement, we spend little time in the office anyway. But 60% commission and office rent too?!" added Panos.

"Yes, I think that was really taking the piss," said Alex.

"It's insulting," added Maria.

"I wonder how long Kostas knew?"continued Panos.

"Who cares. I can't believe they would do that. We are not strangers. For all they know we could have helped.

And honestly, I wouldn't have minded getting less in commission while Nikos sorted out his mess, but not to move into his house and pay office rent." Helen was all steamed up. Luckily, it was just the four of them in the office.

Alex was stood by the window while the others gathered around Helen's desk. He was there for what felt like a very long time, his mind elsewhere as he stared outside. Watching the heads of people going in and out of the buildings into cars, shops or standing around smoking. He watched as the train pulled into the station nearby, letting some people out as more went in. Then his mind went back a couple of Sundays to the Center, recalling the discussion they'd had that night.

"Are we to do the will of the group all the time?" someone had asked. To which the answer was, the individual is the group and the group is the individual. You need to broaden yourself, you need to become the group and let the group be you. The expression of this position in everything brought about unity.

Alex was seeing the teaching play out before his eyes. Society is always separating us. Husband against Wife, Man against Woman, Us against Them. Each person looking out only for their own. We think there is a separation he thought to himself.

Niko must be in a mess and desperate. I wonder how I would have acted. How would I have expressed my individuality whilst also expressing that of the group? he thought. Bringing the situation to the group before making a decision? Is that what being the group means? I guess that would have made everyone included. Surely, that must be the right position he concluded.

Everything was clear for Alex. His relationship with his parents, siblings, the opposite sex and his colleagues. The state of each one, whether "good" or "bad", had to do with his lack of group consciousness or otherwise. Deep in thought, he counted the number of times his ego had got in the way. When he had been selfish in his decisions.

"We all agree Niko handled this situation badly. But I kind of know where he is coming from, the point is, what shall we do now?" Alex turned to his colleagues. "Are we going to carry on with Nikos? What would you all like to do? Should we go for coffee in Kifisia tomorrow to talk about it properly?"

"I think that is a good idea" said Maria.

The deep blue

They had come to Korfos for a long weekend. Alex, Voula, Katerina and the kids had arrived late in the evening. Katerina had stayed back to tend to the kids while Alex and Voula walked to Enplo Bar to meet the others for coffee. It was unusually quiet at the bar, which was great for the group, apart from the mosquitoes which were lethal at that time of the night. Andreas had been talking to them about fear and holding back. He was looking at Despina as he spoke, but they knew he was talking to everyone.

"Good evening," the owner, Nikos, greeted them. "What would you like to drink?"

"An espresso for me," Voula replied.

"Hot chocolate for me, please," Alex said.

"Nikos, what is the fishing situation?" Andreas asked.

"Not encouraging, very little about. The guys saw some dolphins the other day. Must have scared the fish away."

"Oh, we were thinking of going fishing tomorrow. Maybe we'll fish for squid or octopus instead."

"Yes, why not," replied Nikos, before crossing the street to get the drinks.

"Like I was saying... Fear is what keeps people from living and experiencing life. We build barriers to protect, but this protection also confines us. You cannot do both. You cannot live in a cage. To live life is to love life and everything it presents."

"Are you saying we shouldn't be afraid?" asked Alex.

"No, it is okay to be afraid. Like the waves of the sea, it too is a current. It comes and goes. The point is not to let the fear overwhelm you, to keep you from living. To be alive is to take part in life. We prefer to stand at the edge and watch because it means we don't have to do anything. But this is not a healthy position towards life." And so they carried on talking late into the night.

The bay of Korfos was at its best, quiet and serene. The sun had been up for about an hour or two, which made its rays still gentle on the skin. Alex was in his swimming trunks, standing on the deck of Café Pilos, staring at the sea. Voula was seated on a chair putting on her blue snorkel fins. The beach was quiet at this time of the morning, dotted with only a handful of grey-haired men and women who found an early morning swim pleasant.

Voula walked to the edge of the shore, holding her mask, and stood with her back to the sea.

"Come in!" she called out.

"In a minute," Alex replied, but kept looking over the sea. Alex had always loved water and the ocean, even though he wasn't that great a swimmer. There was something about the sound of the waves crashing on the shore and the expansive nature of the sea that filled Alex with peace.

Few minutes later and Alex was knee-deep in water, ready to surrender to the calling of the sea and of course Voula. He dunked himself into the waves, as one would dip a biscuit into a glass of milk. His head reappeared, then went under again, a little longer this time, before popping up next to Voula. Until today, Alex had only swam on the surface apart from the odd dive here and there. He was too afraid to dive deep down to the seabed. But Voula was going to help him with this, and that was why they were there: for Alex's sake.

Voula had first walked through the doors of the Center thirty years ago. "I was afraid to live at the time," she told Alex. "I thought life was miserable, full of chaos. It was difficult at the beginning, accepting what I was taught at the Center.

"It was not until the teachings settled within me and I started to apply them in my life that everything around me changed and my life became a joy. If you embrace the teaching and put it into practice, you will see it's effect over time," she told Alex. "You will find life meaningful again. My life became a joy just by virtue of my exposure to these teachings."

Voula juggled family life with a high-level financial career. However, her life revolved around the Center. She was one of its oldest members. Listening to the fascinating stories of the older members gave Alex hope and strength. Knowing that someone else had walked in his shoes and come out on the other side singing and dancing was encouraging. They were an example of what was possible.

Alex had never experienced anything like it. The different sizes of fish, from tiny and almost invisible to dinner-size. Then there were the colours, some so beautifully co-ordinated you could not but be amazed. The urchins lodged between rocks and the plants that had made the seabed home. Life in the deep blue was something else. They had been diving for an hour, coming up every so often to catch their breath, Voula always nearby, showing Alex a few tricks underwater.

He could have carried on but was tired, partly due to his fitness level but more to his overdose of excitement. Alex felt alive, different and changed by the experience. A big smile drawn on his face, he walked towards Voula, giving her a long loving hug. Voula was in many ways everything to Alex, and her partner Andreas too. He could not express how much they meant to him.

They both sat on the white plastic deck chairs, sipping on freshly squeezed orange juice and drying out in the sun. The beach was now busy with people, young and old. The sun was also in full swing, blaring down on the row of sun-seeking bodies that had spread out along the shore-line. As Alex sipped on his remaining drink, he woke up to what he had heard the night before and what had happened earlier in the day. He had learnt to dive to the bottom of the sea.

By taking a plunge, he experienced more of the sea than he could ever have imagined. You never see anything at the surface, just like you don't experience life sitting on the fence, he said to himself.

"Voula," he said, turning his face to her as he spoke. "I'm ready to take part in life, ready to experience its richness."

"Bravo Alex!" she replied with a smile.

Είναι και Έτσι

Alex and Panos were good friends. They first met at CPG 5 years ago, but it took the unexpected closing of the office for their friendship and bond to flourish. Besides spending their days as estate agents they also had a number of common interests in football, cooking and fitness training which made their time together interesting. Panos used to live in Chalandri, not too far from where Alex lived, but had to move back home to look after his mother who was ill and getting old.

Panos spent the working week with Alex in Agia Paraskevi so he didn't have to do the 220 kilometers trip it took to drive back to his parents' home in Patra every day. Alex, on the other hand, lived far away from family and was happy to have Panos stay with him during the week. Alex was not fond of being alone in the house. He found it still uncomfortable, triggering memories of his relationship with Athena.

Alex had finished early that day and gone for coffee with a friend in Kifisia when Panos called.

"What should we have for dinner tonight?" Panos asked.

"I'm open. What do you feel like? I don't think we have a lot at in the fridge," said Alex.

"Okay, I can do some shopping. Unless you want some souvlaki?"said Panos.

"I think I will be happy with cooking something. I'll see you in a bit," replied Alex.

Alex was at the front door fiddling with his keys when Panos walked up behind him with both hands heavily-laden with groceries. Luckily, the two-bedroom flat they shared was in a block that had elevators, unlike most of the other older buildings in the area. The building was built by the best friend of Alex's dad who was a well-travelled engineer and at the time had built a very modern building with all the mod cons that were yet to become popular in Greece.

Panos decided to cook that night and was going to prepare spaghetti with red sauce and some spinach pie which they could have as a snack later in the day or with their morning coffee. Panos, although a good cook, was always messy. Alex on the other hand was the complete opposite, very tidy in everything he did, cleaning up as he went along.

"What can I do?" asked Alex, offering to help as he cleaned the remnants of chopped onions, spinach, parsley and crumbs of feta cheese spread all over the small breakfast table by the door to the balcony.

"Do you want to cook the spaghetti?" replied Panos.

Alex placed a pack of spaghetti in a pot of boiling water with some salt, adding a dash of olive oil.

"That is not how to cook spaghetti. You should add olive oil at the end, after the spaghetti is cooked," Panos objected.

"Says who? Come on, Don't worry," Alex said, taking no notice. He was more concerned about the hungry noise coming from his stomach as he had eaten only two slices of toast the whole day.

They sat at the dining table with its view of Ymittos Mountain and the shine of the moonlight. Alex was stuffed and was teasing Panos about the spaghetti and the way it was cooked. Then he remembered Panos had complained sometime ago too about him not putting lemon juice and vinegar in his chickpea soup. Like today, Panos had protested, saying that was how it should be eaten.

"I find it strange that sometimes you can't see that there were many ways of cooking and eating a particular meal," said Alex. "Remember the popular Greek saying: 10 million Greeks, 10 million opinions?"

"Yes, of course. I used to hear my grandfather say that to his friends," replied Panos.

"Well, then you know there isn't one way to everything" said Alex. "There is also a phrase I picked up from the Center. It is 'Είναι και έτσι'*. It is a fundamental part of the teaching, because it teaches openness and acceptance. It also teaches us to be in union with everything."

Panos knew how important the Center was to Alex and had visited a couple of times. He had also read a couple of books published by the Center. There was one book in particular, "The Master" which he found very revealing. He couldn't put the book down until he finished. So he knew some things about the Center and where Alex was coming from.

"I think the spaghetti was nice. Besides the food is all going to get mashed up in our stomach whether we put olive oil before or after," Alex said.

"Ha ha ha, very funny. I know what you mean, I guess you could say am stuck in my own way of doing things," Panos replied.

---

* "Είναι και έτσι" in Greek means "It is also like this".

"Sure, we all are stuck on our ideas. You could say mine is keeping everything clean and tidy. But you know, ever since I heard 'Είναι και έτσι', I now think about the essence of things more. Actually, the more I think about it the more I see the problems in the world is down to everyone functioning in 'my way is the only way' mentality. When in reality there is no right or wrong way per se. There is only your way and my way. You know what else we talked about at the Center some weeks ago?" Alex said

"What?" asked Panos

"Being in union with everything. Understanding that life is expressed in many different ways and focusing on the essence, because the essence is the core, the principal thing," Alex said

"That is interesting. But how do you be in union with everything. What does that mean?" asked Panos.

"I'm yet to fully grasp its meaning, but what I understand is this: we don't have to do something in order to be in union with everything. We already are, the only thing we need to do is to wake up to the fact and acknowledge it. Deep, right?" said Alex.

"I would be lying if I told you I understand what you just said now. But anyway, I get what you mean by not getting stuck on certain ways and allowing things to flow naturally," said Panos.

Self observation

It was one of those days when the square of Agia Paraskevi took on a different look. Apart from the walkways running through, every other space was taken by flowers, people and kiosks. The park had been transformed by the many different colours and scents released into the air. It was the first day of May. Like everyone else, Alex was celebrating spring with the festival of flowers and had decided on a walk to the square.

You could see Mount Ymittos from the main balcony of Alex's apartment. You also saw a lot of roofs, solar panels and hot water tanks which Alex did not like very much. But the plants and flowers were going to make the view more pleasant. Alex potted the last plant, placing the medium-sized olive tree in the corner next to the table. The melia flower was on the wooden center table in the living room.

The Newgate clock above the fireplace had just turned eleven. Lunchtime was a few more hours away for Alex, but he was peckish and decided to prepare a snack in the meantime. He took a bite from the cheese toast, which was still hot, before placing it down on the plate. He then flipped open the engraved cover of the journal he'd bought six months ago and started reading the thoughts now crystallised on its pages.

It took him some time to start writing. At first he did not know what to write or where to begin, then he became scared of what might come out. He took another bite of the toast, this time a bigger one. He felt vulnerable putting it all on paper. He tried hard to hold back those thoughts he could not bring himself to confront, choosing instead the general and less penetrating. But he quickly realised the exercise was pointless if he didn't go all the way. It never crossed his mind that it was going to be a difficult task.

Andreas had told Alex everything starts with self-observation. By observing your self in all of its manifestations, your hidden power and the ways you can express it were revealed, he said.

The question *Who am I?* Was followed by *What I know to be a fact.* Along with a host of answers where, *many of the things I worry about are physical and temporal. I came to this world with nothing and I will leave with nothing.* Alex's attention was held by the words further down the page: *as I have grown older I have become restricted, unadventurous and unenergetic. I have allowed myself to be shaped by society into another Zombie.*

He flipped a couple of pages. *Annoyed at the way people drive, park their cars. Dad called today, just to hear my voice he said – a rare act. Quite happy about it, but became concerned for him. Thinking why is he calling me. Is he okay?* On a separate line were the words: *I notice am trying to prove myself right.* A bit further down the page are the words: *It's pointless being annoyed at the way people drive, it's silly and pointless complaining about anything. It's pointless being overwhelmed by other people's actions. Worrying about what people say or think about me.*

He turned over few more pages while taking the last bite from his toast and continued reading. *The decision to entertain a certain type of thought or feeling is my choice. I have to take a conscious decision on what is good for me at any present moment and to be mature about it. It is my choice to feel guilty, pressured, worried etc. I can choose not to entertain these thoughts and feelings.* The next words were starred as a reminder of what Andreas had told them. *Harmony comes from observing and expressing yourself freely without regret or punishment towards the Self. Be brave enough to play all the roles inside you, but consciously.*

The contents of the journal meant a lot more to Alex now. Recording his thoughts and feelings every so often had had a huge effect. It allowed Alex to take a step back and really look at his life at a particular time, focusing especially on his thoughts, emotions and body. This brought him clarity and helped release the tension, anger and ideas within. He was also calmer and had a more positive perspective on life. He had never learnt about writing down his thoughts and feelings before. Not this way anyway. He was used to internal conversations instead.

Something even more special happened when Alex started observing and journaling. He could see his life become free-flowing. Even his clients started to comment about the sense of calm around him. The days of being anxious to closing a deal were becoming few and far between. He did everything needed to get the deal, but wasn't stressed out about the outcome. He found he was doing less identifying and more experiencing. Letting go became easier. Letting go of the stories and false realities he and the people around him created.

Self-observation was a term Alex had not paid attention to until he started going to the Center. He came to know about it early on, sometime during his first month. It was one of the first things he was told and taught. He could remember when it happened like it was yesterday. He had just returned from London the day before. It was about 7pm on Sunday. They were seated in the main front room with Andreas, about seven of them. Andreas had told them, "Self healing begins with self-observation." The words struck Alex immediately.

He had spent the previous week in London attending to medical appointments and visiting family. The blood disorder had been with him from birth and had affected his daily life for much of the time. Sometimes bringing him excruciating pain. His health was still an issue, although much better than he had ever known. However, he wanted to be completely healed. So hearing that self-healing began with self-observation, he had to pay attention. The opportunity to heal the body and make it glow with health was something Alex was keen on realising.

"For each one of you," Andreas continued, "the closest person you are in constant contact with is your own self. By knowing yourself in depth, you acquire a deeper knowledge of what a human being really is."

"If you want to find a dynamic way of living, existing and accomplishing, you should first learn who you really are, being aware of your capabilities and weaknesses, limits and the way these can be widened." Alex found this intriguing, Who am I? What do I believe in? he thought.

"Self-knowledge is beyond getting to know the separate self, rather it is about getting to know the self of the whole of humanity," Andreas said.

"Because when you truly know yourself, then you will have known everyone else. You will recognize the feelings I have; the fears your wife expresses or the joy your neighbour feels. The people and their outer covering may be different but everything else is the same," Andreas concluded.

The first thing Alex did on his way to work the following day was to stop by the bookstore. And on the top of the first page of his journal he wrote: *Self Healing Begins With Self-Observation.*

There is no other

It was 6am. Alex sat on the side of the bed, put on his slippers and pulled the mosquito net over his head before opening the door to his hut. He stood on the outdoor deck looking out to the wild forest thirty meters away, while monkeys played in the trees around his hut. This had been the norm for the last two weeks, waking up to the sound of nature. That was the fun bit; the difficulty was going to sleep at night which was made almost impossible by the bush babies who were just starting their day at that time and seemed to have a lot to talk about.

Alex's first day in Shimba Hills was full of mixed emotions. His initial excitement of being on African soil, receiving a free historical tour from the warm and friendly driver who had picked him up from the airport, quickly turned to irritation at sweating profusely from the heat, and finally anger at not being able to sleep, trying desperately to tune out the noise made by all the nocturnal animals. Sleep came only when he surrendered himself, remembering why he had made the trip in the first place.

The last year had been rough. Everything that could have gone wrong did. The proverbial light at the tunnel was nowhere to be seen. Alex was at his lowest, nothing made sense anymore. Putting an end to it all had become a frequent thought. But then his treasured hobby of travel came to the rescue, together with the telephone conversation with Yiannis. He was going to get out of Athens, from his environment, and the dark cloud which had cast a shadow over him.

Knowing wild animals were a short distance away from where he slept was mind-blowing for Alex. One of the caretakers at the lodge had showed him and the other guests the footsteps of a lion near the perimeter the day before. This got them all excited but worried at the same time. The thought that passed through Alex's mind was that while it would be nice to see the King of the Jungle, not whilst they were walking up the hill to the village school, which was a good twenty minutes away on foot.

Helen filled up the cups with porridge while Alex arranged them on the concrete platform in the kitchen ready for the youngest children of the school who filed into three lines for their morning breakfast.

"Jambo!" Alex and Helen said, waving to the kids.

"Habari za asubuhi," they replied in unison as they waited patiently for their turn.

As well as trekking up to ten kilometres just to get to school most of the kids went without food too. How did they do it, where did the strength come from? Alex wondered. Especially on an empty stomach. He could not remember ever walking that far to anywhere.

Besides the programme set up to feed the children at least one meal a day, Alex and the other volunteers constructed wooden tables and chairs. They also built new structures for the school toilets. The latter was the toughest part of the experience, as Alex and David had to push wheelbarrows of red sand up a steep slope leading to the school in baking sunshine.

"If only we could do this task later in the evening when the sun was less punishing," Alex said to David, as he pushed the beaten barrow and its wobbly wheels up hill.

"That would be nice, but the school would be closed by then. Being close to the equator must have something to do with the sun's intensity," David replied.

There was also a lot of playing around with the kids. Two of whom were Ibrahim and Jumapili. Ibrahim wore an oversized school uniform and was almost lost in it. He had a grown-up face, seeming to have experienced so much at such a young age. He was also confident and curious at the same time.

"What is your name? Where are you from?" he asked Alex on their first meeting.

"My name is Alex. I am from Greece, what is your name and how old are you?" Alex replied.

Ibrahim was five and came from one of the neighbouring pastoral villages. He had an older brother in the same school. Jumapili on the other hand was playful and full of smiles, like the Sponge Bob character on the dirty yellow top she wore to school. She was always making faces.

"Can I see?" she would say, leaning over with her friends to see the photos Alex had taken from the day before. "Can you take me too?"

"Yes, why not," Alex replied before taking a few shots.

"Let me see, let me see." She rushed back. "What does that do?" Pointing to the menu button by the viewscreen. Jumapili was fascinated by the digital camera and the experience of seeing herself in what looked like a TV.

Their comical faces and playfulness made Alex laugh. Something about the energy of the kids helped him break free from his melancholy, allowing him to see life as something beautiful once more. The children, although poor, still managed to bc happy.

The table was full of all sorts of local and continental

food. It had palm wine too, which was the first thing that caught Alex's eye as he and others walked into the dining room. Simon, the lodge manager, had promised him the wine. It was their last night in Shimba Hills and Kenya; within 24 hours Alex would be back home in Kifisia, Athens. As he chewed on his chapatti and sukuma-wiki, he thought about the last month's activities, the children he had built a bond with, the serenity of the forest and what lay ahead.

Alex had started going to the Center just before he travelled to Kenya. The place was still new to him and so he did not say much whenever he went there. He was still self-conscious too. What he did do was listen. After he returned, he found himself listening to Andreas talking to the group about the need to help others as they journeyed through life. He said by helping others, they were helping themselves.

In the room with the group that evening was Mrs Klairi, a graceful old lady with an oval-shaped face and long silver hair. She had been a member since 1980 and was one of the first people Alex had met. He had never known anyone so dedicated. She spent every evening at the Center performing healing for people who asked for help, and had done so for thirty years. Alex caught a glimpse of her as Andreas spoke, her infectious, warm glow radiating towards everyone in the room.

Andreas said people spent too much time fussing about their own miseries, forgetting the misery of others was also their own. "Besides," he continued, "we need to realise that there is a common nature to all people. When we understand this, we realise we and the others are one." He told them serving others was not a duty or obligation but rather helped realise unity. And this had a magical way of bringing healing to both the served and the server.

As Andreas carried on talking, Alex's mind went back to Stephen Kanja Primary School and his time in Shimba Hills. He realised as he sat there that his compassion for and time with Ibrahim, Jumapil and the others had carried his depression away. He'd thought he was helping the kids, but it turned out it was the children who had helped him heal.

Seeing children as little as five go without breakfast, then walking barefoot for kilometres to school was more of a concern than his own depression. His own problems seemed so small and almost a joke compared to what the children of Stephen Kanja Primary School had to go through daily.

Alex had not made the connection until then. Serving and doing so selflessly was a form of healing with profound benefits to everyone.

Change/Harmony

Alex was walking to the station on his way to work when he looked up at the sky. It had rained sometime during the night. The sky was cloudy while the temperature was mild unlike the previous three days, which had been foggy and cold. As he passed through the barrier to the station platform he thought how quickly the weather changed from one day to the next, and how life too mirrored this change.

It was 7am. The train was packed with commuters as usual. Finding a seat was impossible by the time the train pulled up at his station. Alex and the six other people who got onto the section of train took to their position, which was to stand throughout the train ride. Looking around the carriage, his eyes met with the typical scene of headphones in ears, phones and tablets in hands, and a handful of people reading a book or the morning's newspaper. But most were absorbed by their electronic toys, which he thought had taken over a lot of people's lives.

"We have four appointments this morning Alex. Two in Marousi, One in Drosia and the last one in Ekali," said Panos

"Great! They are cash buyers, right?" asked Alex.

"Yes. Have you spoken to all the owners?" continued Panos.

"Yes, I have, they are all waiting for us. And I have the keys for the house in Drosia, so we can do that viewing anytime," replied Alex.

It seemed he'd barely got down to work before it was home time again. He could not believe how smoothly and quickly his day had gone. Very different from the day before, which had been unusual to say the least. As he shut down his laptop and started packing up, the brief nature of things popped into his head again. Everything, it seemed, was passing, the manic events of yesterday to the calm of today. Even his experiences were short-lived. Lost in thought he wondered if there was a way to make certain things in his life permanent.

The alarm went off the next morning. His face was

on the pillow while his hands stretched out to stop the alarm clock on the bedside cabinet. Reluctantly he rolled out of bed, took off his pyjamas and dragged himself into the shower. His brown eyes sprang wide open as the cold stream of water from the shower hit his body. He held his body under the cold water for about 5 minutes before turning off the tap. He had arranged to meet with Maria for coffee at Platonas before heading to the Center later.

They sat in the corner by the window. Next to them were an old couple and their grandson, as was evident from the little boy's call out for "Yaya!". Maria was in an unhealthy relationship but was afraid of the change that was to come should she leave her partner Thanos. Where would she start at her age, she told Alex. Starting anew was more disturbing than staying in an abusive relationship. She was comfortable though not happy.

Alex had always seen Maria as a strong woman and found it difficult to understand why she could not make the decision to leave. "We have gone past clinging onto something that is not working," he told her. "Besides, there are lots of men out there."

"Yes, but it's not that easy to start dating again. Besides, where will I meet a guy?" she replied.

"I think we look at this things the wrong way. Don't worry about where, just focus on healing yourself and being open to life and you will find miracles do happen," Alex said

"Why do I always attract this type of man?"

Alex knew this feeling; he'd had similar ones many times in the past. Finally, Alex told her of the messages and little thoughts that had popped into his head and which they had also discussed during his various visits to the Center.

He told her about movie night at the Center, when they'd been going to watch The King's Speech. Every so often, a movie was watched and analysed for its hidden wisdom. This was one of the many ways Alex and the other members got a better understanding of the teachings. Whilst waiting for more people to arrive, some of those already there started talking about the economic crisis and change taking place in the country. The conversation had carried on for a while when Andreas intervened, telling them they were getting carried away by the superficial and in the process missing the essence.

He told them life was a wheel in constant motion and people were at the periphery of it. "Because we are at the perimeter, we cannot see everything. All we do most of the time is just live and experience some parts of the life. But life is always teaching us to grow through everyday events. The questions we should be asking are, what can we learn from this crisis? What does this crisis teach us as a country, group or individual? How do we broaden our consciousness?"

He carried on, "Broadening our consciousness makes us more aware, moves us closer to the centre of the wheel, the center of life. And when we reach the centre and we stay there, then we see the whole wheel, the whole of life, the essence of life."

Maria did not say much and was still trying to make sense of what Alex had said. "Let me tell you what I understood from that evening," Alex continued. "At the moment we are at the edge of life. Sometimes life spins very fast and other times slowly or at a steady pace. What we want to do is slowly move to the center, to the point of harmony, where we can watch, learn and grow through our experiences of life without feeling overwhelmed or lost.

"Like you, I also wish some things in my life could be stable. But I realised something the other day through the weather. Life is change. Like the clouds that are constantly moving and changing from one day to the next. And you know what?" he asked her. "The situations in my life vary like the weather. But the essence I have found was in the position I took with my experiences, trying my best to see the truth and not get wrapped up in the chaos or even calm, as this also very quickly changed."

"You are right," Maria told him, "but it is still difficult."

"Of course it is. I know that. But I also know we cannot let fear stop us from moving, from living life. We have to be in union with life, which in itself is constantly changing."

"You know I have been where you are now and it really isn't that bad. It feels difficult and impossible, but it is not. We just have to sum up the courage to embrace change. Besides, the longer you stay with Thanos, the more his obsessive and aggressive behaviour hurts and damages you emotionally."

As they finished off their coffee and motioned to the waiter for the bill, Maria remembered the words written on the front page of a book given to her by her father for her birthday. It read, Harmony stands in the middle of experiencing all things.

"You see? Your dad has already given you the message," he said jokingly.

Knowing

Alex could hear the locks turn one after the other until the door opened.

"Hello Alex! Come in."

"Thank you, how are you?" Alex asked.

"Hectic. I've been running around all day," said Penelope.

Alex opened the living room door to find Litsa playing on the floor with her dolls. "My dad bought them for me," she told him. Beside him stood Penelope gazing happily at her bundle of joy, amazed at how quickly she was growing. Alex watched this dainty princess, her gleaming teeth, jet-black shoulder length hair and infectious smile which lit up the room. The pains of the past seemed to be a distant memory for Penelope as he could tell from the wide smile on her face.

"Where is everyone?" he asked.

"On their way," she replied.

Alex and Penelope had started their self-study group on the same day. Both had stumbled upon the Center through what at the time looked like a tragedy that had turned their world upside down, stirring up a deep quest to find a meaning to life. They were forced to turn towards the path of self awareness. Their stories were very similar, helping them forge a close bond, which over the years had grown stronger.

Penelope had met George at the University of Brighton, where they were both studying engineering. It was at the library where George made his move for the fair lady who had captured his attention. Their early years together were like a fairy tale. They studied and played together, laughed a lot and were almost inseparable. George was two years older than Penelope which naturally meant he graduated earlier. He was also fortunate to get a job with a multinational company, but this required him to make frequent trips abroad.

George's travels made Penelope insecure. And although she was happy for him, she preferred how things were before. She was certain she was going to lose him if she didn't do something. George had just returned from one of his trips when she broke the news of her pregnancy to him. She was 6 weeks in. George was beside himself, not knowing what to do. Then he became angry and blamed her for letting it happen and for trying to hold back his life and career. No matter how hard Penelope tried, she could not salvage the situation.

What had happened to Penelope 5 years before was that everything fell apart. Although she had finished her studies, she had lost George. Her life's course had changed. Her career was on the back burner and raising a child as a single parent in London was proving difficult. And so she moved back to Greece to live with her parents and found work as a mathematics teacher at the local school with the help of her uncle.

The Center had become a key part of Penelope and Litsa's life. Penelope had come to know of the Center through one of their summer seminars. She was still hurting at the time, hurting from the pains of past mistakes, and was desperately searching for a solution for the sake of herself and her daughter. She was sceptical at first, but this quickly changed when one of the group leaders she spoke to during the event told her, "We decide which feeling we want to entertain in our lives every single moment." Following this with the question, "Do you want to choose to be well or unwell?"

Her breakthrough came on a weekend morning when she had gone with Alex, Despina and a few others to help clean the Center. They were taking a break on the small rear veranda by the kitchen when Andreas walked in.

"Would you like a coffee?" Penelope asked. She made him a double shot of Greek coffee, and together they all sat talking. Then she summoned up the courage to ask a question which had been on her mind for some time. She asked him how she could overcome paying for the mistakes of the past. A mistake she said was affecting her life.

Andreas was silent for a while. But this seemed like eternity for everyone and especially Penelope who may have wished she had kept quiet. Andreas took a sip of his coffee, which was now bearable to drink, then answered her. "There are no mistakes. We are only ignorant. The decision you made at that time of your life was based on what you knew and believed. Realising it was not a wise decision later should not mean beating yourself up over it. You don't need to judge or punish yourself over and over again. If you knew better you would have done better."

Alex thought at the time how profound those words were and told Penelope so afterwards. It lifted a weight off his shoulders, he told her. "How often do we keep punishing ourselves over something we said or didn't say or do?" Alex was quite apt at that. He would spend days whipping himself. "But here we are, being told there are no mistakes, only a lack of awareness of the truth."

"Only now matters," Andreas said. "There is nothing to pay for. There is only ignorance and knowing. The moment you know, you forgive, and then you move on with what you now know. When you forgive yourself, you free yourself. And only then can you and your daughter be well. The important thing is to love yourself." He had not finished speaking when tears started to trickle down Penelope's face.

"I know I have to do what you say but I don't know how I can do it," she blurted out.

"No, you don't have to do what I say, it is not a command," Andreas replied. "Nothing we say here is a must or command," he said, turning to the group. You should know that by now. Just sit with the idea, let it fill you and see, really see through meditation if it makes sense, if it is true for you."

Litsa was going to turn five in a few days, and to mark the event Penelope was throwing a party for her princess. They had also just moved into their own home, so the celebrations were for both occasions. Alex opened his bag, handing Penelope a housewarming present. She unwrapped the gift to find a frame bearing the words We are not required to do anything but to live in the Now. Then he handed Litsa her present, to which both celebrants responded with a thank you, before Penelope placed the wooden frame on the wall above the fireplace.

Let's go fishing

All Alex could see was the various shades of brown rooftops and the outlines of houses, big and small, surrounded by the green of the hills. He could also make out the cars and restaurants lined one next to the other. Then there was the sandy shore, which now looked like a thin strip before the shimmering blue sea, and the wake of bubbles and waves left behind by their boat. In front of them was the vast, soothing expanse of the sea and the raised heads of Akgistri and Egina islands at a distance.

Kostas and Pavlos were sitting an arm's length apart on the left, while Alex was a little to the right at the bow of the boat. They were all facing Andreas, who had one hand on the throttle and another on the strap securing him to the boat. Apart from their captain, everyone had a reel whose silver lines and bait were some meters deep, luring the unsuspecting fish of the Saronic Gulf.

The sun had by now travelled to a point where its warmth and the gentle breeze of the open sea was refreshing to the skin. As they cruised at about 5 knots further away from civilisation, Pavlos reeled in his bait then dropped it back into the sea again while Alex tugged his line every few seconds while steering out at the open sea.

Pavlos was short and stocky with receding hair. He also wore a thick moustache which added a kind of maturity to his appearance. He had the kind of face that stopped you in your tracks. Pavlos was handsome all right, but inside he was beautiful. Add to that a big heart, something Alex had noticed in his early days at the Center, and found admirable.

Although his family was only three years old, he seemed to be settled into his role as husband, father and breadwinner with relative ease, though the latter was proving more difficult. He and his wife ran a second-generation export business of olive oil products.

"Andreas, I have this thought that everything seems to be blocked or slowed down," said Pavlos.

"What is the matter?" replied Andreas.

"I don't seem to be able to close two of the deals I have

been working on since late April, and I don't know what to do. It is beginning to get to me, especially because of their value and potential to be recurring clients. I know we are advised to be unattached to the outcome of our work and to take part consciously," Pavlos said

"We all have that problem. Of trying too hard," Andreas said. "You know... Work is a form of meditation; a ritual to be offered to the Entity. We work for a result, we ask the Entity for the specific result we want, but we are not attached to the outcome, because the results do not come from us but from the Entity, the call is with Him. The point for us is to be in the flow of life, to work knowing that what we do is part of the universal meditation, taking place in everything, everywhere and in every moment. When we start thinking we lose the essence and start worrying and before long we become stressed."

"How do we work without being attached to the outcome?" Alex asked, expressing his own difficulty with the concept.

Silence was everywhere around them, but there was so much going on. Some dolphins were at a distance playing. Bubbles formed as fishing reels sliced through the water. They were nearly two miles from home.

"If we look back in time, we will see that none of the results we have achieved were by our doing. We put things into action, just like we are doing now. But we never created the result. We cannot make the fish come to us. We can only set down the bait. And like I said before, our work should fulfil us, we should carry it out as a ritual not as a compulsion," Andreas said.

"The issue is one of being in harmony and trust. The fact is that there is no way for God to abandon us. He has always come through. All our worrying is down to forgetfulness and ignorance. We need to align ourselves with this truth, but every minute. Otherwise we forget and lose focus", Andreas continued.

Alex had been out to sea with Andreas many times before and had come to know these trips were not so much about fishing but about clearing the mind. Catching an octopus, squid or fish was a gift, as had been the case when Alex caught his first fish. He had not felt the weight of his catch and was surprised when he pulled in the line. The lavraki, as the sea bass was called in Greek, appeared to have come to him. Before then, Alex had been eager to catch something and even prayed silently, but he'd always drawn a blank.

It was just like the time he was in East Stavo, Kenya. He had gone on a safari with the group he was volunteering with in Mombasa and then too everyone was eager to see the "Big Five", and especially the king, the lion. The gift of seeing a pride of lions came only when they were rclaxed and not thinking about it. They were actually looking at a herd of impalas at a distance when someone turned to see the lions. It was here Alex really understood that no matter how much people tried, they could not force things to happen.

Pavlos was silent, creating space within him for what they had just heard. Pavlos' silence was interrupted by what seemed like a tug on his line. He pulled to be sure, but there was nothing.

Suddenly, it dawned on Alex that life's struggles where actually a means to finding resolution within the Self. Struggles come up for us to work on them, he thought.

The journey back to land was swift, the boat at full throttle as they raced pass one of the few open sea fish farms in the area. Mooring the boat took a bit of a skill from Kostas thanks to the tailwind tossing it left to right like a child's plaything in bathwater. Lunchtime and the ensuing afternoon nap closely associated with Greek life passed so quickly that soon it was night.

This light of mine

The church was packed to the brim with people and so were the courtyard and the streets leading up to it, standing one next to the other, old and young alike, all holding candles, some fitted with plastic wax catchers, others with makeshift aluminium foil. All of different sizes and colours, the candles like their owners waiting patiently for the clock to strike midnight. Amongst the chatter he could hear the priest's voice through the loudspeakers and the bangs and whistles of fireworks, some letting out colourful smoke while others contended with the stars in lighting up the night.

Alex was standing next to Kostas and his son Niko. Immediately behind them were the rest of the group. It wasn't long before the whole crowd started reciting the ritual prayer of Paschal Troparion in unison with the priest as the minute hand of the clock edged closer to twelve. The prayer ended with a sounding of the church bell and the simultaneous bangs of fireworks. "Christos Anesti!" ("Christ is Risen!" in Greek) rang through the air as the gathering exchanged kisses on both cheeks with their friends and loved ones.

The candles' wait was over too as they kissed one to the other until each was lit with the holy flame from inside the church. Ending a journey which started in the church of the Holy Sepulchre in Jerusalem some hours before. The candles were now the center of attention as the people walked back to their homes with cupped hands protecting the flames from the wind.

"We will go and drop off the candles and meet you at Andreas' shortly," Kostas said, as he and Niko turned left towards their house, leaving Alex to walk the short distance between the two houses. On getting to the top of the stairs Alex met Odias, the stray cat sitting patiently by the landing, waiting for dinner. Besides, Odias, there was also the cross on the soffit over the front door, made with the smoke from the candle as was customary, a new addition to the scene.

"Alex, can you cut the Easter bread and distribute it on the table."

"Yes, Voula," he replied.

"And this too." Passing him a basket of dyed eggs and a bowl of salad.

"Who wants Mayeritsa?" cried out Voula, as she dished out the traditional Easter soup one after the other to their respective owners. The other option was an egg lemon soup which Alex never liked. Rice, tomato and cucumber salad, slabs of feta cheese, spinach and cheese pies and meatballs followed the starter. In between the chatter and munching was the battle of the strongest egg.

"Where is your egg?" Alex asked Despina with hands stretched out, egg steadied, the pointed end ready to do battle, the latter succumbing as the two clashed heads. "Next!" Alex called out, as Kostas stepped forward with his egg. Kostas had already knocked out Niko, Voula and a few others. So the game went on until the strongest egg was crowned and celebrated with an uproar.

When they had finished clearing away after dinner, Alex, Kostas and Andreas retired to the balcony, from where they had an unobstructed view of the shimmering sea.

"Goodnight, and thank you," said Niko, his small head poking out of the sliding insect net screen.

"Goodnight, Niko," responded Andreas, followed by Alex.

"I'm walking home with Mother," Niko said, directing his words to Kostas, who nodded in acknowledgement.

"Andreas, I realised something when we were walking home from the church earlier," Alex said.

"What?" asked Andreas.

"The whole ritual with the holy flame; It seems to me the light of the candle is the light within each one of us."

"Good, I'm listening," said Andreas.

"Well, when we were lighting the candles one from the other, I saw it as, us giving the light we have to others, helping them light up their life?"

"This is very good," said Andreas. "Everything is symbolic. When we draw a candle we do not only draw the flame, we show the radiance too. The ritual is a reminder to the people, to let the spiritual light within radiate out; to let their light shine."

"How is it going?" asked Voula, as she and Despina joined the group, sitting on the two plastic chairs they brought back to the balcony where they had been taken to make up the numbers during dinner.

"Alex was sharing his thoughts about the holy flame with us," Kostas replied.

"As I was saying, it is good to stay connected to the essence of these rituals as you have done, and not get carried away with celebrations. The same applies to marriage and other key events. Marriage is a blessing and about the inner work of union, not only about making babies or raising a family," continued Andreas.

But how and why, do we get carried away, Alex's thought slipped out.

"Do we get carried away because that is the easy option? Because then we can pretend and don't have to do the work? Or is it because we don't really know the essence of these things?" Alex asked.

Alex, Kostas, Voula and Despina listened as Andreas responded. "It is easier to get carried away. It doesn't involve any work or commitment. Letting the light within shine requires work, inner work, unfortunately nobody wants to do this work. The irony is this is the real work we have to do."

Fly on the wall

The rays of the afternoon sun peered from behind the half-closed window shutters of the apartment, making its presence and heat felt as they settled down for the ritual afternoon nap. Alex, slouched on the sofa, had taken off his t-shirt exposing his Buddha belly for all to see. It was Alex's fifth time in Nafplio. He and Despina had come to visit her parents for the long bank holiday weekend.

He rubbed his belly in a circular motion, thinking in a few hours they would be back in Athens. Then he noticed the extra kilo or two to his slender frame, thanks to Eleftheria, Despina's mother, and her constant plea for him to eat. "Fae*, Alex! You must eat" she would say with his every meal. Not that Alex minded, as every dish she had ever cooked was delicious, especially her stifado with orzo.

Eleftheria and Yiannis were in the corridor by the kitchen door, hugging each other for what seemed like eternity. Alex could see them from where he was sitting. He had never seen anything like it before. A few days before, it was Despina who was doing the hugging, first with her brother and then her dad. Alex looked on, trying to make sense of what was happening. His girlfriend's parents hugging each other freely and openly without a care in the world for their guest. Recalling the events of the past days, he realised quickly that this was not a show for the guest but a natural everyday occurrence in the Peppas household. Expressing love and affection was the other side of the hot and fierce Greek temper he had come to know.

What had started many years ago was starting to make sense. At the time Alex was in a relationship with Athena. She was the first one to ask him for a show of affection outside of the bedroom. Alex didn't understand what was asked of him at the time but obliged anyway, though reluctantly. He actually made fun of it on numer-

---

* "Fae" in Greek means "eat"

ous occasions, thinking it was not a manly thing to do. It didn't take long for the same issue to raise its head in his relationship with Despina. This time he knew better and did not resist but still did not understand why until now. As he lay on Despina's bed, staring at the white ceiling with its glow in the dark moon and star shaped plastic, everything became clearer.

Athena and Despina asked Alex for what they had always received at home, the expression of affection. For Alex, this was somewhat alien and rarely seen in all of the time he'd spent at home with his parents and siblings. He knew his family loved him but this knowledge was not openly expressed or reaffirmed in any physical way. Seeing Yiannis and Eleftheria playing cards, Despina wrapping her hands around her mother's shoulders and Yiannis giving her daughter a peck on the cheek, helped him see and understand where his partner was coming from.

Alex's family relations and upbringing was clearly different from that of Despina or Athena. He knew that now. Alex sat up on the bed for a while then walked to the kitchen where Despina was washing the plates from their lunch. Standing behind her, he wrapped his hands around her, squeezing firmly. She turned, surprised and wondering what was going on, but said nothing. He was quiet too, and there they stood in a warm embrace.

Alex was keen to talk to Andreas about his weekend and could not wait for evening to arrive. He had arrived early to take part in Chorodromena before the group sessions started. Chorodromena, as taught by the Society was a kind of dance, with symbolic movements that balance the energies and forces in and around us. Dancing was something Alex had liked very much from as early as he could remember. But this dance was different. It was dancing with total awareness of the movements made by the body.

Chorodromena taught the members to broaden the boundaries of the self, to convey and be in union with the universal dance expressed in all creation. Alex loved Chorodromena very much. The tingling of energy it sent through his body. The sense of calm and enthusiasm for life. He also liked that it helped him clear his mind and prepare for the night ahead.

The late night's discussions unfolded in the small front office where the members spilled over from the room into the opposite waiting area and the adjoining stairs. They must have been about twenty in number, including Alex, who was perched on the windowsill with his right shoulder resting on the reveal.

"Andreas, why does it feel difficult to express affection and how come some people show affection easily and others don't?" Alex asked. "We never had that kind of environment in my family, but even then, I never came out feeling unloved or unwanted. I don't know about my brother but for me, I knew my family and friends loved me and that was enough. I know people and families are different, but still I am a curious."

Andreas was sitting opposite Voula, his legs crossed and stretched out under the desk. "Why do you think that is so?" he asked the group, but no one answered.

"You are right that every person and family is different. And there could be many reasons why we chose not to express affection especially to those close to us. What we should remember however, is that, every parent raises their family the best way they know, and from their experience of how they were brought up.

"When we look deeper we will see that our parent's actions stem from their love and need to protect. Even if they go about it the wrong way, the original intention is love. People are afraid to express their feelings and show affection because they think they may get hurt. But in reality, the pain is bigger when you keep your emotions and you don't express them. Then the emotions are trapped inside us and this brings greater suffering."

"But Andreas, what about if it doesn't matter to you, or you express your affection in a different way?" asked Kyriakos.

"Well, it is the same thing," Andreas replied. "If it doesn't bother you, why are you holding back? Some people are afraid that if they express what they feel, they may lose something. What they do not know is that the reason why they are afraid of losing something, is because they are expecting something from the others. But when you see and acknowledge the Entity in the other person, then you show your feelings and affection without expecting anything in return. Then you have nothing to lose. What is there to lose, when you are not expecting anything from the other person? Do you understand, Alex, does it make sense?" Andreas asked.

"Yes it does Andreas," Alex replied.

What do you see?

Alex was on the 4:15 train heading home after a busy day at work when a lady boarded the carriage he was in with her two daughters. One was about four years old, the other probably just over six months old. The train was at Dafni, one stop from its starting station, and was not yet packed with rush hour commuters. The freckle-faced lady sat down opposite Alex, her older daughter choosing to sit in front of her mother, beside him. The little one and her buggy were next to them, away from the vestibule and aisle.

The two girls were pretty and animated as any little children of their age. The older girl had long caramel hair, almost reaching her lower back and was dressed in pink pants, a white flowery top and matching hairband, swinging her legs back and forth as if seated on the edge of a swimming pool. Her chubby-cheeked sister had big, beautiful eyes and hair gathered together with a purple rubber band. Her pushchair was adjusted so she was almost sitting, allowing her to add her presence to the occasion.

At some point during their journey, Alex caught sight of the baby looking at him with a smile on her face. She looked with such intensity, her gaze penetrating every fibre of his body. Somehow, he knew she was really looking at him. He could feel the gleam of recognition in her eyes. Her warmth and love. Their meeting was intimate, beyond the train and its passengers. And though brief, was more meaningful than the whole day's prior events.

The train pulled up at Agia Paraskevi, Alex's stop. He got off as more people scrambled onto the train. He stopped by the fruit and vegetable stall just outside the station for some groceries, exchanging a few pleasantries with the owner before making his way away. Then the questions popped into his head, one after the other. What if God wasn't somewhere far away but was right here next to me or in front of me? What would happen if God was at my level, in my everyday moments?

He set the bag of groceries on the kitchen table and poured himself a glass of cold water before sitting down, then returned to his questions. It would really change things wouldn't it? If God was in everything and everywhere. Funny thing is, on one hand we are told God is omnipresent and on the other we act like he is in some faraway place we call heaven. If God is omnipresent, then he must be in my neighbour Tania or my colleague Helen!

How would I treat them with this knowledge? How would I react to their many aspects, some of which I like and some I don't? How different would it be to see beyond the outer covering of the people or events I encounter every day? His experience with the baby girl on the train was still with him. That little girl, he thought, looked beyond my mask and its many layers. She probably saw God in me. Suddenly, a lesson he had received at the Center a few months back became very clear.

It was a Monday. Alex had been at the Center since 7pm, when his self-study group started. The discussion within the group that day centred on awareness, a topic unknowingly continued in the bigger group on creative meditation, which started around 10. Here they were about thirty in number and this time led by the Head of the Center. One of the psychologists in the group, Dora, had expressed the difficulty she experienced connecting with her clients, all of whom were drug addicts.

"I sometimes find it difficult to help my patients," she proclaimed. "I can't seem to connect with them without being patronizing. My mind is always stuck on criticizing their behaviour. I really want to help but I don't know how."

"Dora's cry is true for everyone," Andreas responded. "We limit our awareness and so cannot really help each other or live a fulfilling life. Without awareness, all we do is see individuals, differences, egos, identification. So the drug addict is just that, a drug addict. He is different from you. He is a pain to you, his family and society. We have identified him as hopeless, irresponsible and placed him in the many boxes we create. But when we are aware, we realize there is something else beyond the body – consciousness, Entity, God, whatever name you want to call it. We begin to realize the commonality between you and the addict. And with this everything changes, you operate from a position of love, of unity."

"What we learn here is how to see the Entity in everything," Andreas told the group. "When we do, then our interactions and their quality become different."

Alex thought about what he just heard but could not make sense of it. "How can I see God in a drug addict?" he asked.

"Andreas, how can we see God in someone who hurts us?" another person asked.

The lesson was simple, but difficult to take in for everyone in the group judging by the many questions raised. But they knew they had to be open to what was said for its understanding to be revealed. They ended the night with a meditation on total and complete interest in everybody and everything.

Still sat at the kitchen table with his glass of water, Alex jumped back and forth between that evening at the Center to his afternoon encounter with the baby in the train. It all made sense now. The baby was innocent, her mind pure and free. She could only look at that which Alex was, his essence. There was nothing else for her. And it was this expression of unity from the baby which touched Alex and left him feeling good. Dora and everyone else, on the other hand, had forgotten this truth, this way of looking. Only the outside, the layers were seen. What lay beneath had been covered up.

Finally, he arrived at the answer to his questions. God was indeed in his everyday moments. He only had to look with awareness to see Him in everything, everywhere. Then he remembered a quote from one of the books at the Center. It read: What exists, visible and invisible, is nothing more than the projection of the Entity's Essence.

Etimo!

The magical atmosphere of the season was about the place. The excited smiles of children warming the frosty air as they chased each other around the room. The girls in pretty dresses and the boys well groomed in their shirts and trousers. The grownups were dressed for the occasion too, as was Alex in his white button-down shirt and navy blue trousers.

The tree was 5 feet tall, snow white in colour with silver streaks. Seated on top was an angel holding a big silver star as if pointing to the sky. Deep red and golden balls dangled off its branches. Its lights swirled around from top to bottom. Nestled next to the TV at one corner of the room, the tree looked so beautiful it caught your attention the moment you walked in.

New Year's Eve was a wonderful time of year for everyone, made special by the gratitude of seeing one year come to an end and the joy of going into a new one full of surprises. It was also one of the times when many of the Center's members gathered around the dinner table. A table that could easily have spanned 7 meters if set in a straight line, one that on this occasion sat twenty-five people. Of course, there was a separate table for the kids, not that they sat down to eat.

Alex could not help but notice the everydayness of the teaching, and its application, as they worked in unison at setting the table. He placed the cutlery, while Maria, the host, arranged the plates. George and Pavlos took charge of the wine glasses. Then there was the strategic location of each breadbasket, salad bowl and the various dishes cooked by the members brought out from the kitchen by Sofia, Voula and Nicky.

The aroma and marriage of colours from the dishes were tantalising. Meatballs, stewed beef, pan-fried pork chops and stuffed chicken wrapped in bacon, followed by rice, pasta bake made with cheese and ham, spinach and cheese pies, boiled and fried potatoes. The variety of salads ranged from Greek to the light-hearted tomato and cucumber, to the heavy, laden with fruits, nuts and bacon. Then there were the desserts set on a smaller ta-ble adjacent to the kitchen wall. These had chocolate and cheesecakes, baklava, mini fruit tarts and the famous milk pastry unique to Greece.

"Etimo!"* shouted Maria, ushering the pockets of peo-ple scattered around the house to the table. Alex was with Pavlos on the balcony of the 9th floor apartment, looking out into the night sky and the festive lights span-ning the streets.

"Alex, come sit by me so I can be sure you will eat," said Andreas, while Nicky joked, asking if Alex wanted to swap, referring to their body frame.

"Wine anyone?" said Voula as she poured the con-tents of the keg she had brought from her dad's vineyard into Alex's glass.

In between the busy mouths were burst of laughter and smiles as everyone ate merrily. Plates and dishes crossed hands and tables like spaghetti junction in At-lanta. Through the generous chatter, Alex motioned to Sofia for some more meatballs and rice. The meatballs, it seemed, were a favourite as there were only a handful left.

"Chronia Pola!" Voula said, raising her voice and slow-ing her words, prompting a harmonious response from everyone followed by the kissing noise of raised glasses. And then an exchange of warm embraces by everyone as they ushered in the new year.

---

* "Etimo" in Greek means "Ready"

The tables were gone and the chairs were resting along the walls by the time Alex came back from the rest room. Traditional Greek music streamed from the speakers as the cakes and desserts were dished around the room. Then To Poulaki Tsiou came on and soon the middle of the room became a dance floor. The Greek version of the Italian Pulcino Pio song had been released during the summer and was a hit with everyone thanks to it's engaging lyrics and catchy beats. Led by the children and followed by Voula, Alex and Maria, pretty much everyone graced the dance floor as the night went on and the music moved from old to new, pop to rock, soul to folk. The night ended at the Center which was only a few minutes' walk away from Maria's house. There the group gathered for a short meditation as was customary for welcoming the new year, before all heading home.

It was a wonderful crisp January 1st. The sky was clear with very little clouds. They were sat in the courtyard at the Center talking.

"I felt heavy when eating one of the dishes from yesterday," Despina said.

"Really?" asked Pavlos, "I thought the food was tasty."

"Me too. I thought they were all nice," added Alex.
Then there was silence as they waited for Andreas to speak.

"What do you think?" Andreas asked, directing his

question to the rest of the group with him. But all of them gave different answers.

"People confuse tasty food with good food. We nourish the body through food, so the food we eat is important. Food is also energy and its purpose is to give energy. It is not meant to make you heavy, tired or sleepy," he said. "There are three things when it comes to food: the food itself, the utensils and the person cooking the food. Food should be fresh, with little spices and sauces, as these two reduce its vibration."

Raw food! Alex thought to himself.

"Utensils should be clean, and finally, there is the cook and his or her state of mind when the food is being prepared. Do you know why a mother's food is always delicious to her child?" he asked them. "Because she cooks from a position of love for her child and family. This love goes into the food. This love is what nourishes the child.

"And what happens when she is upset, moody or angry? The same food is not as sweet, because all of her being passes into the food."

"Oh, I have been there. Many times too. The same food tasting heavenly some days and horrible on others. But I never saw it that way or paid attention to my mood when cooking," Alex waded in.

"Yes, we all have. And this is because we don't pay attention. It is almost automatic. No presence or awareness in what we are doing. What we are eating, how we are when cooking," Andreas replied. "But there is something even worse. Fast, ready-made or canned food. The process involved in preserving these foods kill the vibration and energy of the ingredients. All they do is fill our stomach, but they do not give us the energy the body needs."

"Is that why I sometimes feel hungry after only eating a few hours before?" asked Pavlos.

"It could be. We don't need to eat a lot of food. We just need to eat the right food to stay healthy inside out and have the strength to do the work we are here to do."

"But how can we avoid eating canned or ready-made food, especially these days?" asked Despina.

"The point is not so much in avoiding these foods, but in the awareness of the importance of food, how it is cooked and our state of mind when cooking. Of course eating as fresh as possible is ideal," Andreas concluded.

A new dimension to food and life, Alex thought as he listened to Andreas give them examples of how to improve their energy intake even when eating fast or ready-made food.

"What do you think?" Alex asked Despina as they walked home later that afternoon.

"It's an eye opener for me," she replied.

"Yes, but I think we might struggle a bit with the fast food. That means no more souvlaki," he said jokingly.

"Funny. You say that but that is something we could

easily stop eating. Even you complain it is heavy and sometimes gives you a tummy ache," she replied.

The birds and the bees

Alex woke up early that morning. He was internally reciting some mantra as he lay in bed. Then he rolled on his side, bringing his face about an inch from Despina's. He tried not to wake her and just stared as she slept, fixated on the shape of her beautiful lips. Gently, she opened her eyes and placed her hands on his. He smiled at her, she smiled back, and started caressing his hands. He leaned forward and gently kissed her on the nose, before moving to her forehead and finally to her lips.

Despina was on her belly now, her head resting on the pillow while her hands were tucked away under it. She liked it when he kissed her. He usually started from her neck then slowly moved down her body until he reached her toes. He liked kissing her that way too and especially enjoyed getting her tickled when he got to her waist. She felt his breath on her as they faced each other. She watched him, whispered in his ears before pulling him closer to her, kissing him with her plum lips. Soon the music between them became a symphony carrying on long after the crescendo which set their bodies trembling all over.

Despina's head was on Alex's lap while he sat up on the bed, his hands running through her frizzy hair. Alex had come a long way. His Mr International days, a name given by his friends because of his history of dating women from pretty much every continent, were in the past. Looking back, he could see the change. He'd thought he knew what it was all about back then. Now, he knew he had not known a thing. He always cared about his partners, and how they felt, but now everything was different. There was a lot more to it.

Suddenly, in mid-thought Alex turned to Despina and asked, "Did you feel anything just now? Something happened to me. I feel full of energy and content at the same time. And I have this thought in my head."

Despina looked up into his eyes, asking him to carry on.

"I think I just found something out." His body still buzzing as the current of energy raced through. "I have been carrying on like an animal all this time, until now. It's not about the number of rounds is it? Or pounding away for the sake of orgasm. That is very much like dogs or rabbits. But we are not rabbits are we?"

It had been difficult for them in the beginning. Their habits and the ideas they had created around them from years of acquired knowledge from the outside world made creating a new perspective tough. But they persisted, sometimes together, other times out of sync. Now they were seeing the change. Their new outlook was starting to show them a glimpse of the two becoming one.

"It really does change everything, doesn't it?" Despina answered. "I feel the same way too."

Alex did not know what to expect when he'd started going to the Center, and certainly did not expect to be taught about sex and making love. Sex wasn't something he usually associated with spirituality, the same as everyone else. But that was where the Center had been very different for Alex, Despina and the many people who went there day in, day out. The Center's motto, "Spirituality in everyday life", gave it all away. From serving others to making love, the spiritual essence in everything was the focus and what they learnt to put into practice.

Alex's change in his attitude towards sex had started some months before on a chilly winter evening. They were seated in the courtyard, the gas burners in the background, keeping the cold out. There were about sixteen of them including Andreas. They gathered around in a circle, and the conversation started with one of the couples in the group.

"You guys are not having enough sex," Andreas said.

Alex thought he'd heard wrong and was a bit uneasy with the topic, but then Andreas carried on by asking them what sex was about. Of course, no one answered.

"If you think sex is reaching orgasm and rolling over to sleep, then you have no idea," he said. "Sex between couples is a ritual. Like everything else: eating, talking, singing, dancing, writing, walking, working and so on. They are all rituals to the Entity. And if it is done with this awareness, then it becomes spiritual, it becomes healing. It becomes union with God. But we don't see it that way and that is the problem. Do you know why people get tired after sex? Why the next thing they want to do is sleep?"

Again no one answered. Alex, like the others, waited for the answer.

"Because couples are not aligned. There is no reference point to the partner's Entity. It is just a mundane task to satisfy the senses. The man and woman are there but not there," he said. "The mind is elsewhere, on the next task, on tomorrow and worse, on another woman or man. If our focus is on the body and the genitals only, then it is pointless. It has to be more than that and it is more than that."

Alex and the others received many more insights that night, and although not everything made sense to him at the time, he was open to what he heard. And now seated on that bed, Alex and Despina were experiencing what they had been taught seven months earlier. For Alex it was a feeling of being alive. Even as they spoke he was buzzing as if an electric current was passing through him. The other thing he experienced was the feeling of oneness with Despina. He had never felt like that before. It was like she was in him and he in her. It was a powerful experience for them both, one which showed the power of the teaching they were receiving and how every little thing in life could be experienced not as a routine but as a miracle.

Where are you?

In the morning, Alex had shown an apartment in the trendy neighbourhood of Politia. The husband was a footballer for Olympiacos Football Club, while the wife raised their two-year old son full-time. They were a lovely couple; the husband, Yiannis, however, had an agent who wasn't to Alex's liking. He wasn't expecting a football agent to be involved in the negotiations of renting a property.

Alex had rented properties to sports men in the past but had never dealt with their agents until now. Yiannis and his wife loved the apartment; it had everything they wanted, was of minimal style, and had a view to die for-

-you could see almost half of the northern suburbs of Athens.

The problem was not Yiannis or his wife, or the property owner for that matter, it was the agent. He was driving a hard bargain, wanting to win on all fronts, which could not happen because Maria the owner had been in the game for a long time, and there was demand for her properties. She wasn't going to sell short to an aggressive agent.

Alex was hoping Yiannis would step in, since he and his wife wanted the flat, but he didn't. He probably didn't want to go against his agent's negotiations. The situation was not going too well.

"We will take the property for €5,000 cash upfront and sign for 1 year," said the agent.

"I am not too concerned about paying upfront. The listing price is €7,500, as you know, and I cannot rent it for the price you are offering, not for a one year contract anyway," the owner replied.

The unpredictable outcome made Alex uneasy. He'd already made plans for the thousands of euros that was to find a home in his bank account – his rent for the next six months, servicing and changing the fan belt of his car, and enjoying the little luxury of a short break in Ithaca.

Lying in bed later that afternoon, he realized that his mind was a few days ahead of reality, and though he knew it, he allowed his mind to daydream. He stopped soon after, realizing the futility of it all. He got up, had a shower, and ate his favourite meal, spaghetti with keftedakia. He never tasted meatballs made better than Greeks.

Maria opened the door just as Alex was about to press the bell. She must have seen him through the glazed panels. A sense of calm came over him the moment his foot stepped into the building. He exchanged greetings with everyone in reception including the two women in the waiting area, then walked through the kitchen to the courtyard where many people were seated and talking.

Andreas was sitting on the white sofa. In front of him on the coffee table was a box of mini ice cream cones. It was Thanasis' name day. Alex greeted him with a kiss on both cheeks, then helped himself to one of the frozen desserts. He had just sat down when Andreas asked, "Where are you?"

"I'm here Andreas," Alex replied. Anyone who didn't know better would think it was just a simple question. But Alex knew better, he had been asked that question many times before.

Questions like this popped up repeatedly at the Center, sometimes addressed to someone specific, other times to everyone. But always, they were never just simple questions to be answered with one word or a sentence. They were also frequent because they served as a reminder.

That was something Andreas did, he always reminded you, so you could act on whatever it is, because it is very easy to forget, to get carried away.

The first time Alex heard the question and the discussion that followed, it was directed at Kiriakos. It was a question that had a deeper meaning, one that asked, Are you here in this present moment or are you elsewhere? Kapou allou, as they say in Greek.

Even when it was not clear to the eyes, there was this knowing, either from Andreas or one of the older members. They knew and could feel, when you were not together. When Alex first started going to the Center, staying late to hear the discussions he used to wonder. How does he know what is going on in each person? It took him sometime to realise how. He found out one evening when Andreas, addressing the group, said, "you need to have the other person inside you."

It is this position of total care and union with everyone at the Center that gives Andreas and the older members this knowing. Just like a mother feels when her child is not well even though both are miles apart. So Alex was in dreamland, and Andreas was here to remind him that life means the present moment. Life is what is happening right now. The action is right here.

"How do I stop my thoughts distracting me?" he asked Andreas. "How do I shake off the habit of entertaining every thought? I find it difficult not to think."

"Well, that is another problem," Andreas replied. "Too much thinking. You need to form the habit of remembering to stay in the here, all the time. At the moment, thinking and dreaming if I can say so, takes you away from your present experience. And this is what brings suffering. To be totally here, is to be alive, to be living. To be in the past or the future is to be "out" of life. People like to dream all the time. That way, they don't have to do anything. They are busy doing nothing. But then you are not alive, you exist, but you are not living." This reminded Alex of what Paris, the leader of his self-study group, had shared with him once, of the monkey mind, which jumps from one thing to the other instead of staying still and focusing on the here and now.

Alex had heard it all before and knew Andreas was right. He had to let go of the monkey mind and practise being absorbed by the present experience. Being in the flow of life as it played out.

You can open your eyes now

The last couple of months had been rough for Alex. The dejected expression on his face had become unshakeable following the loss of Athena. His mind and health had taken a heavy toll, his mind more than anything else. He was at that place where he could not find what to live for. There was no meaning to who he was or wanted to be. Somehow, surrendering was the only thing left after his phone call with Yiannis. And following that was the question: what to do? Fortunately for Alex, another good friend of his, Bubu was in town about the time the question arose.

They met for lunch on one sunny Thursday afternoon in June. Alex picked her up at KAT station in his blue VW Polo, and together they drove to the restaurant in Stamata. She was looking stunning as usual, this time in a free-flowing purple dress. Bubu was a real woman, shaped like a figure eight. Her olive green eyes and jet black hair had her turning heads every time. Alex was certain she had caused a few accidents when she walked down the street. Her beauty on the outside however was no comparison to who she was on the inside.

Odysseas Taverna was located on Stamata's central square. A rural suburb on the outskirts of Drosia. Alex chose the area for its clean air and greenery. He had first visited the taverna with his colleagues for their office Christmas lunch. The aroma of grilled meats greeted Alex and Bubu as they walked up the short flight of stairs, promising a wide variety of pleasures and a full belly. They sat in the open area, shaded by a couple of olive trees. Alex knew what he wanted to eat, leaving Bubu to scan through the menu handed to them by the round-faced, chubby waiter.

They munched on fresh grilled bread and boiled greens over meaningful talk while waiting for their main course. Bubu was happy to be back home. She had missed the sun's nourishing rays, and of course the food. The grilled bread drizzled with olive oil and a sprinkle of oregano was already threatening to fill her up from its taste and freshness. Alex was happy too, but in a different way. Bubu's joy had an effect on him. But how? He could not tell. For now, he was happy just being out of the house.

Alex was in the middle of pouring out his heart when the waiter turned up with their paidakia (lamp chops), fried chips, fried courgettes, salad and a slab of feta cheese. Have we ordered too much food? was the expression on Bubu's face. The stack of lamb chops alone worried her. Alex, on the other hand, was quite hungry and looking forward to the challenge. His mouth watered from seeing the dishes set before them. He squeezed three half lemons on the lamb chops before helping himself, then carried on telling Bubu about his despair.

She ate and listened as he talked. She waited until she had finished chewing the last piece of courgette before telling him about a spiritual center she'd stumbled upon twelve years before. It was called The Servers' Society (Omilos Eksipiretiton). She said it was a special place and they could help with his health, psychology and more. She told him she would have been lost too had it not being for her finding the Society. He thought about it for a minute then said to himself, "I have nothing to lose. I am already at the bottom; the only direction now is up." And so he decided to take Bubu up on her offer.

Alex was on the phone to Bubu, checking whether he needed anything else for his appointment at the Center that evening. He had filled in a form the week before telling them about his concerns. She told him not to worry, there was nothing else needed. He just had to turn up at the appointed time of seven. As evening drew closer, his mind started turning over thoughts of what to expect. What would they do? How would they help him? Would they cure him? His mind rambled on until it was time to set off.

The Society was located in an area of Athens known as Agios Eleftherios, on Nine Sarantaporou Street. Like many of the narrow streets in Athens, this one ran from a local train station on one end to a busy central road on the other. The first thing Alex noticed as he walked up the street was a high-flying Greek flag erected on the first floor balcony.

The building was white, two stories and of the 1930s. Alex stood outside the building feeling nervous about pressing the bell. When he finally did, a curly-haired woman greeted him, inviting him into the waiting area. She asked him a few questions then disappeared upstairs into one of the rooms. Alex felt a strong sense of calm descend on him as his eyes roamed around. But he was also uneasy at the same time, not knowing what to expect.

The woman came back down, sitting behind what looked like the reception desk. His eyes turned to the display of books on his right and then to the painting on the wall in the room to his left. He looked back at the woman behind the desk, thinking how beautiful she looked with her frizzy brown hair. Then she motioned for him to follow her, leading him to the room in the far left corner at the top of the stairs. In the room was a graceful old lady, probably in her seventies. With her were another lady and gentleman, both much younger.

The older lady introduced herself and the other people in the room. "Can you tell us a bit about yourself and the things you wrote in the form?" she asked him. Alex responded by giving a summary of his health and state of mind. She then explained a few things. She stood up, walking round her table to where Alex sat. She then stood behind him. "Please relax and close your eyes", she told him. With eyes closed, Alex wondered what was going on, his mind and body restless with anticipation. Then suddenly he felt a tingling in his body. First at the top of his head, then his feet. He felt this sensation rise up from his feet. He could feel his heart beating through his whole body, its pace steady. That was what he could remember. His eyes closed for about twenty minutes.

"You can open your eyes now."

He did not want to. He wanted to stay where he was, experiencing the calm and peace that rose up within him. She smiled at him as he opened his eyes. He felt refreshed, woken up from sleep. He told them how he

YOU CAN OPEN YOUR EYES NOW

felt, the tingling sensations around the top of his head and its movement from his feet upwards. She said that was very good and smiled. They exchanged a few more words before he thanked them and left the room. On getting downstairs, he booked another appointment for the following Tuesday with the lady at the reception as instructed.

He felt free now, at home. He started talking to the receptionist. Her name was Despina. She told him how long she had been in the Society, about Mrs Klairi, the older lady upstairs, and more about the work of the Society. She asked how Alex found the Center, what he did for work and where he lived. She said it was a good thing he'd encountered the Center, and was sure everything would turn out fine. Alex smiled, saying he hoped so. He then thanked her and said goodbye.

Alex headed back to the station thinking about his first session of spiritual healing. He could still feel the tingling sensation through his body. He thought about how it felt so secure being in the building, the warmth and purity of the people he had met. He wanted more of this feeling. He wanted such an environment in his life.

Crossing over

It was no coincidence the Center was located on a street named Sarantaporou, for "Poros" in Greek, meant to pass from one place to the other. Crossing over was something one had to do the moment he or she decided on making the Center a part of his or her life.

Omilos Eksipiretiton - The Servers' Society was started by a poet and philosopher named Dimitris Kakalidis. A simple man, who following his own personal journey of awakened spiritual consciousness set out to help others realise their Higher Self. A man who taught by example, revealing the spiritual essence of things through simple and everyday activities people could understand. He was known as "Daskalos" (the Master).

It was from the same building where Alex and the others now gathered that the Master taught. It was here that people gradually gathered around him, many coming from far and wide. From the reputable to the common man, and also men and women abandoned by society. He embraced all equally, seeing beyond their personal limitations. Rather he saw their potential and true nature, a position which was now gradually expressed by everyone who had come to know the Master and his teaching.

Among the wider group of people who visited and spent many of their days at the Center were an even smaller group. People who wanted more of what the Master had to teach. They drew closer, spending day and night with him as he passed down the wisdom of the Entity that exists within everyone. They became his disciples, learning first-hand how to express their Higher Self.

The Master saw everyone as a complete entity without limitations. The total belief by the Master in the people who came to him made it possible for them to be, see and do things differently in a way that transformed their lives completely. A change that brought about harmony regardless of the ups and downs of life itself. He taught them to see the essence of life, to express it in their own unique way and to work for the good of everyone.

So the disciples, in parallel with learning and putting into practice the teaching they received, began to serve. At home, in their places of work and within the community. Soon, expressing spirituality in everything became a way of life for them. With this came the ability to heal and help others, which is the work of the Society. This was how Alex came to know of it and be a member.

MEGAS SEIRIOS PUBLICATIONS
Greek Editions

Dimitris Kakalidis

- The Wisdom of the Poem
- The Wisdom of the Short Story
- The Hidden Lotus of Revelation
- Fallen Paradise Holy Matter
- Logos the Third
- Incentives I
- Incentives II
- The Revelation of the Entity

Klairi Lykiardopoulou

- Woman - Exploring her Position and Role in Society
- Man - Exploring his Position and Role in Society
- Couple - Exploring its Position and Role in Society
- Spiritual Healing, *A human potential in theory and practice*
- The Master [1], *First Concepts – First Experiences*
- The Master [2], *The Awakening of the Soul*
- The Master [3], *Processes of the Mind*
- The Master [4], *Accomplishment – Spiritual Healing*
- The Knowledge of the Educator
- The Power of the Woman
- Man and Money, *A philosophical study of their relationship*
- Individuality Unity Monad
- The Family Circle
- The Sacred Task of the Soul
- The Heart of the Earth, *Imaginary Short-stories to give Light to our Planet!*
- The Diachronic Master [1], *Seeking the Knowledge in simple thoughts and deeds*
- The Diachronic Master [2], *Discipleship in the Eternal Truths*
- The Diachronic Master [3], *The Power of Love*
- The Diachronic Master [4], *Our Hidden and Apparent Self*
- … And the Shadows became Light

MEGAS SEIRIOS PUBLICATIONS
English Editions

Spiritual Healing,
A human potential in theory and practice
by Klairi Lykiardopoulou

The Master [1],
First Concepts – First Experiences
by Klairi Lykiardopoulou

The Path from Fear to Fearlessness
by Ioanna Dimakou

Individuality Unity Monad
by Klairi Lykiardopoulou

Seeking… from Alpha to Omega,
Synthesis of Science and Philosophy
by Mina Gouvatsou-Karekou

The Revelation of the Entity
by Dimitris Kakalidis

I will be here
by Paraskevi Kostopetrou

Small Temples on a Wave
by Vassiliki Ergazaki

Experiences of a Spiritual Healer
by Kiki Keramida

Ade Durojaiye

"You can open your eyes now" is the first published work of Ade Durojaiye. When Ade is not writing he is busy refurbishing properties as his day job. Ade currently lives in Richmond, England but spends every available free time in Greece with his spiritual family. You can contact Ade using the details provided overleaf.